# LILIES AND CARNATIONS

A play by

Liz Lees

Lilies and Carnations
A play by Liz Lees

Published by Green Light (Manchester and Edinburgh)
Ilkeston, 6 Chelford Road, Old Trafford, Manchester M16 0BE

Cover Printed by Indigo Lithoprint, 1/18 Bridgewater Centre, Robson Avenue Urmston, Manchester M41 7IL
Printed by MARC, 28-30 Edge Street, Manchester M4 1HN

ISBN    0 9527604 1 X

# LILIES AND CARNATIONS.

## CHARACTERS

**Marjory** - *Fifty, capable, cheery. She is very capable at running a hotel, being polite to guests faces while enjoying speaking about them behind their backs. But she is under a great strain, under which she eventually cracks, breaking all her own rules of behaviour.*

**D.J.Joe** - *Twenty five, lively. A flashy young business man who likes to be in the lime light but enjoys a good time and isn't afraid of hard work.*

**Nesta** - *Fifty five, but seems older. She is a scheming selfish bitter woman who feels that life has treated her badly.*

**Valerie** - *Forty five, tall. She works hard at being attractive. She is excessively aware of beautiful possessions and very nervous to be seen to be doing the 'right', modern, thing.*

**Sidney** - *Sixty eight, with a twinkle. He is a likeable, cuddly old man, who, although widowed, is happy with his lot. He is very fond of Marjory , and is efficiently protective of her.*

**The Man** - *Forty, tall, efficient. He has a job to do, knows he could get abuse so tries to do it as unobtrusively as possible. He quiet likes the look of Valerie, they have the same interest in furniture.*

First Performed At Saxon's, Winsford, Cheshire and subsequently at the Ramada Renaissance, Manchester in 1992 with the following cast

| | |
|---|---|
| Marjory | Catherine Gilman |
| D.J. Joe | Robert Maxfield |
| Nesta | Francine Rees |
| Valerie | Mary Waters |
| Sidney | John Henshaw |

Directed by Liz Lees
Stage Manager Michael Elphick

**PRODUCTION NOTE.**

The setting for Lilies and Carnations is the reception lounge of a local hotel. The action moves rapidly as characters go to and from different areas of the hotel. These areas are clearly defined by lighting changes which draws attention to the next piece of the action without a pause for scene changes.

Costume, set and props are all modern and easily obtainable.

Although written with proscenium arch in mind the play has most frequently been performed in the round with a shallow raised stage in the centre of the performance area. Use is made of every entrance, and screens used to create entrances where they do not naturally exist. The Reception entrance of Act One could also be the entrance to the small room of Act Two and have storage space for props accessible near by.

The story is one of characters, confusion and chaos, with opportunities for audience reaction

# LILIES AND CARNATIONS.

## ACT ONE.

*The reception lounge area near the entrance of the Buckingham Garden Hotel. A few arm chairs and a low coffee table which might have seen better days. To centre stage, a serving hatch or door to the kitchen positioned so that items from the kitchen can arrive without the staff being seen.. There are doors either side, one to the Pagoda Bar the other to the Reception desk. Front stage right the entrance to 'The Orangery' the larger function room, used today for a wedding. Front stage left the entrance to the 'Gazebo Suite' used for today's funerals.*
*Marjory a middle aged woman, is talking to the Receptionist, Angela, who we do not see. Marjory wears a black shirt, smart flat black shoes, a white blouse covered by a bright cardigan. She dumps her handbag and brief case out of sight near the kitchen. She looks into the kitchen and begins to take off her cardigan*

**Marjory** Yes, Angela, it's all here, thanks. Plates for funeral one, due two o'clock. Plates for funeral two, due four o'clock. Plates for wedding, three o'clock. Paper napkins for funerals, linen for wedding - top table only. *(produces paper cup)* Oh dear, not up to our usual standard. ... I thought Rosemary was going to be late. 'You get off to your appointment ... Small Hoteliers or something - I'll cope. I do have some experience after all'.

*Angela shouts from the reception. A man with a clip board walks in and nods to Marjory as she moves from the kitchen*

Oh, you're here. Get on with it if you must, though why you can't wait until five o'clock I don't know. *(checking dishes etc., to Angela )* Going to be a bit short staffed with Michelle gone. We should manage if the breakfast staff have done their bit.

*D.J.Joe enters ready to start work. He is keen but doesn't really know what he is supposed to be doing. He is wearing a frilly fronted white shirt with rather large red bow tie*

D.J.Joe isn't it? I'm Rosemary's Mum, Marjory. You look nice.
**D.J.Joe** 'Nifty Shirts' can always come up with the looks. Like to dress the part. *(he preens himself)*

**Marjory** 'Nifty Shirts' - Your shop, of course! Very nice. ....Right. Are you
      ready?... You have done this before haven't you.*(she removes cardigan)*
**D.J.Joe** Loads of times. Buckingham Gardens trained. You want the music?

*D.J.Joe switches on a cheery pop music at the bar*

**Marjory** Let's go then!
**D.J.Joe** Hey - what's this?! *(he holds up a paper cup)* We can't use these!
**Marjory** Yes, we can - a bit short on crockery.
**D.J.Joe** Someone had a major accident washing up?
**Marjory** Can't explain now. Just get on with it. Are you ready? .... Let's go!

*There follows a mirror image routine, with D.J.Joe copying
exactly the moves that Marjory makes. There is a pile of tables
in each of the function rooms. Marjory starts to set hers up for
the wedding, top table, lots of flowers on tables and around 'The
Orangery'. D.J.Joe does the same in 'The Gazebo'. When
Marjory goes back to the hatch for more items for the tables,
D.J.Joe has a quick look into 'The Orangery' to check he is
doing exactly the same. Marjory always pauses on her return to
her room so that they start moving again at the same time.
They shout to each other as they work*

**Marjory** Table clothes.
**D.J.Joe** Table clothes.
**Marjory** Cutlery.
**D.J.Joe** Cutlery.

*As they lay the tables out, finding a rhythm*

**Marjory** Soup spoon, bread knife, fish knife, main knife.
**D.J.Joe** Soup spoon, bread knife, fish knife, main knife.
**Marjory** Fish fork, big fork, little fork, desert spoon,  ... another fork.
**D.J.Joe** Fish fork, big fork, little fork, desert spoon,  ... another fork.

*Neither of them know what this last fork is for*

**Marjory** Napkins and glasses and give them a polish.
**D.J.Joe** *(quietly taking it in)* Napkins and glasses and give them a polish.

*Marjory has a cloth to polish the glasses while D.J.Joe uses
the next napkin so that they, in turn, end up crumpled*

**Marjory**  Glass polished. Napkin placed.
**D.J.Joe**  Glass polished. Napkin placed.

> *D.J.Joe is following her instructions with great enthusiasm, teasing. She is annoyed because she thinks he is taking the mickey, but becomes amused. Their activity will speed up as each action goes along. As they finish work they meet near the centre*

**D.J.Joe**  Phew! It's a lot to take on, two in one day.

> *D.J.Joe turns music off*

**Marjory**  Well, you can't really plan these things. You get the phone call the next morning you see. And it's the time of year for it. Today's Thursday...
**D.J.Joe**  Odd day for a wedding. All those people having to take a day off for it. Don't know if I'd have bothered. It's my half day and I've a good assistant in Mandy. You'd not have seen me otherwise.

> *Marjory has, meantime, been working out the dates not listening to D.J.Joe*

**Marjory**  Today's Thursday. Now, ... Saturday night, ... Sunday, very cold ... and that fog - finishes them off. And everything's shut, you see, so they are all in rush to phone in first thing Monday morning, and we get it all to do on Thursday. So that's why there's two. ... Lucky it's not more really.
**D.J.Joe**  Weddings??
**Marjory**  Funerals.
**D.J.Joe**  Oh, funerals!
**Marjory**  Yes
**D.J.Joe**  Funerals?
**Marjory**  Yes.
**D.J.Joe**  Funerals!
**Marjory**  And a wedding.
**D.J.Joe**  Not two weddings?
**Marjory**  Where have you been all morning? Two funerals, one wedding. Where are you going?

> *D.J.Joe heads off towards 'The Gazebo'. Marjory follows him. They both stare at all the wedding finery in the funeral room*

**Marjory**  Oh, my god!
**D.J.Joe**  When's the first one due?
**Marjory**  Two o'clock.

**D.J.Joe**  What's the time.
**Marjory**  Five to.

> *D.J.Joe is about to dive in to start gathering cutlery, but stops and looks*

**Marjory**  There's no time.
**D.J.Joe**  No... no...
**Marjory**  Black cardigan! Your tie!
**D.J.Joe**  Black tie! Bow tie for weddings. Black tie for funerals.
**Marjory**  Try Angela on reception.... or the Chef.

> *D.J.Joe dashes off left. Marjory takes another look round 'The Gazebo' and sighs. The man looks in the funeral, decides which to list first, and moves into the wedding. Marjory watches him in despair. She looks at 'The Orangery' and is satisfied, but sighs again. She shouts to Angela as D.J.Joe runs on left and off right*

**Marjory**  You didn't have one? ... Did he tell you what he's done? Set up 'The Gazebo' for a bloody wedding and the first lots due any minute! ... Can't do anything about it.

> *D.J.Joe returns taking off his bow tie and putting on a black tie*

**D.J.Joe**  There!
**Marjory**  That's better.
**D.J.Joe**  What now?
**Marjory**  Nothing. Just wait. ... Doors open round the back for the guests? Only the person who made the booking should come through here.

> *Every thing slows down. She fiddles with a flower arrangement,*

**D.J.Joe**  You are an expert, aren't you?
**Marjory**  You could say that.
**D.J.Joe**  Got certificates and that?
**Marjory**  Yes.
**D.J.Joe**  Years of experience?
**Marjory**  Yes.
**D.J.Joe**  Did you put Rosemary into it?
**Marjory**  *(edgy)* Into what?
**D.J.Joe**  This business.
**Marjory**  Oh, thought you meant the hotel. She got this on merit, you know.

**D.J.Joe** She's good.
**Marjory** I'm glad you think so.
**D.J.Joe** How come you're here today?
**Marjory** She'd to go to a meeting.
**D.J.Joe** Small Hoteliers, like last time?
**Marjory** Something like that.
**D.J.Joe** Her Dad came last time.
**Marjory** Yes, he can't manage it today, so you've got me, O.K?
**D.J.Joe** Fine, yes.

> *D.Joe feels slightly put down. Marjory tries to change the mood and subject*

**Marjory** So, come on D.J., who's Mandy?
**D.J.Joe** My assistant.
**Marjory** That all?
**D.J.Joe** Well...
**Marjory** Rosemary told me! So how's business D.J.?
**D.J.Joe** Good, very good. Huge run on paisley shirts at the moment. Hectic. But I just thought a bloke needs to get away from it all sometimes.
**Marjory** So you come here.
**D.J.Joe** My relaxation, the discoing.
**Marjory** Done waitering before?
**D.J.Joe** No, only setting up and clearing but it's just a matter of dishing out the nosh. Nothing to it.
**Marjory** What?! What about the silver service?
**D.J.Joe** Don't bother with any of that.
**Marjory** You'll have to! - for the wedding! I can't do it all on my own.
**D.J.Joe** With any luck they will be half cut and won't notice. ... I should be setting up the music. Don't know if I've got anything for funerals.

> *Goes to bar to select and put on music, he tries out several*

**Marjory** Taking their time aren't they? *(laughs)* Late for his own funeral! ... We could get that room as it should be.
**D.J.Joe** No time. They could be here any minute.

> *Marjory moves towards reception and shouts to the distant Angela*

**Marjory** Angela? No sign? ... What? How long? *(checks the time)* We've got ten minutes. We can do it.
**D.J.Joe** *(too involved elsewhere)* What?

**Marjory**  Come on, clear the wedding/funeral.
**D.J.Joe**  Why? Has he changed his mind? Decided not to go through with it?

*He goes to clear the real wedding but Marjory heads him in the right direction*

**Marjory**  Wrong one. It's running late. Ten minutes. We can do it. *(removes cardigan)*
**D.J.Joe**  Right!

*Both work on the clearing. The Man moves out of the wedding and off towards reception without being seen by D.J.Joe*

**Marjory**  Leave side plates and small knife.
**D.J.Joe**  Right.

*Everything is collected rapidly onto trays. Some confusion in passing each other and on returning loaded trays to the kitchen*

**Marjory**  Made it! Just the flowers.

*They both load as many vases of flowers as they can carry, come out into the main area to meet a little lady in black. They can hardly see for flowers, so nearly smother her*

**Marjory**  Oh! I am sorry are you all right? *(she carries the flowers away)*
**Nesta**  Me? I'm very well, thank you. I'm looking for 'The Gazebo', young man.
**D.J.Joe**  The..? Oh, the loo. There. *(pointing)*

*Marjory has meanwhile dumped her flowers, gone for her cardigan. Nesta has gone off in the direction of the toilets, which are back towards reception, and returns*

**Nesta**  Are you new here? The man on Reception said it's through here.
**D.J.Joe**  'The Gazebo Suite'?! *(under breath)* Man on Reception? God! Must be blind if she thinks Angela is a bloke!
**Marjory**  Here, this way Madame. Let me take your arm. *(she is putting on her best funeral voice, full of sympathy, but Nesta doesn't need any of it).*
**Nesta**  I can manage perfectly well thank you.
**Marjory**  How are you?
**D.J.Joe**  Fine day for it.
**Nesta**  I hadn't noticed.
**Marjory**  This way.

**Nesta** *(looking into the room)* Oh, very nice. Simple. I like that, with the flowers.
**Marjory** Flowers?
**Nesta** Yes, the flowers.

> *Marjory does a rapid signal to D.J.Joe to replace the flowers*
> *which he does, bewildered*

**Nesta** Where's the sherry?
**Marjory** Just coming. *(aside)* Straight into the sherry.

> *She takes in a tray with thirty glasses of sherry, whisky and*
> *orange juice, puts it down beside her*

**Nesta** Oh, very reasonable.
**Marjory** We are expecting thirty. Is that right?
**Nesta** No. Six.
**D.J.Joe** All that work!
**Marjory** Leave it. It will save us setting up for the next lot. ... We would like to apologies for the paper cups and plates.
**D.J.Joe** Major accident in the kitchen.
**Nesta** Well, it's not the standard I expected here. I presume there will be an adjustment to the bill?
**Marjory** Of course Madame.

> *Marjory and D.J.Joe go off for food behind the hatch*

> *The action moves completely to Nesta who supervises this*
> *small family funeral. We only see her*

**Nesta** Well, Dolly, come in. Find a table. You've five to chose from. This one I think. I know it's paper cups, but we're getting it cheaper. Alexander, don't wander around, just sit down. Oh, for goodness sake Dolly give Tracy a handkerchief! Didn't you equip her with one before you left? Arthur, I know it's her first funeral but surely a handkerchief is a first essential. Dolly doesn't think. *(she raises her voice as she believes Uncle George is deaf)* Uncle George... ... Uncle George ... the toilets are down there. *(aside)* Weak bladder, going just like she did. We'll have it all to go through again with him. ...You don't need the toilet? Well, take your sherry and sit down. Alexander! Don't poke at the jam ... it's marmalade? Are you sure? Very odd, for a funeral. I didn't ask for it. She wasn't particularly fond of it unless it was the kind with Drambuie in it

> *Marjory and D.J.Joe overhear as they move to the door with*
> *the food*

**Marjory** Marmalade?! That's what happens it you let the breakfast maids set up.

**D.J.Joe** In with the sandwiches now?

**Marjory** Not yet. That one hasn't finished by a long way.

**D.J.Joe** Lovely little lady. Coping very well.

**Marjory** Hmm... *(taking food back to the kitchen).*

**Nesta** Dolly, as the eldest, would you like to say a few words, or will I?
Of course it's necessary! I know the vicar said something, but it was all 'Our dear departed sister' - but she wasn't his sister, or ours. Raise your glasses, 'To dear Aunt Polly. Long may she rest in peace'... Someone thump her back. Not you Alexander. Dolly... that's right. Has Tracy never had sherry before? Gin and tonic? That girl drinks gin and tonic?!! *(shakes her head)* Dear Aunt Polly... of course her drink was port.

> *Nesta finishes her sherry and takes another glass. Returning to her speech*

Aunt Polly dedicated her life to her husband, Wilfred. Uncle Wilfred, long since gone. They were the perfect couple, never separated. She went along on all his business trips, all over the world ... ... after some incident that happened in Germany, in 1935 ... ... she swore she'd never let him out of her sight again. ...
That large house of theirs was spotless and remained so ... ... until the housekeeper left shortly after Uncle Wilfred died.

> *Marjory and D.J.Joe have listened to her and exchanged looks. They get ready to come in with the food and coffee but are waved away by Nesta as she takes another sip of sherry and continues*

Of course, then Aunt Polly's life changed. No more lavish entertaining, friends drifted away. For a few years she wintered in South Africa, ...
... spending a lot of Uncle Wilfred's money, until I had a word with her. Aunt Polly was never 'aware'... wore that mink coat of hers right up to the end, despite the shouted abuse in the streets. Though why you didn't take it off her, Dolly, I don't know. She lived in a world of her own , ... and that large house.

> *Marjory and D.J.Joe are a bit at loose end. They can't take food to the first funeral because Nesta won't let them. They hear Angela shout from reception, they hear a car draw up and they leap into action. The Man moves from Reception through to the kitchen.*

*D.J.Joe sees him.)*

**D.J.Joe** Excuse me Sir, you can't go through there, it's staff only.
**Marjory** Leave him, D.J. Angela says the wedding car's arriving.
**D.J.Joe** Tray of drinks. Who is he?
**Marjory** No time to explain now. Not that tray - that's for the first funeral.
**D.J.Joe** All look the same to me.
**Marjory** They are the same - only that ones has got the lacey cloth so it's the wedding.
**D.J.Joe** Right. *(changes tie)*
**Marjory** You doing this one? *(taking off cardigan for wedding)*
**D.J.Joe** Right.
**Marjory** Go on then.

> *Marjory goes forward to the Orangery to meet the bride and groom who have come in the back way. Her tone is now bright and cheerful*

**Marjory** Ah! The happy couple. First of all I would like to apologise for the paper cups and plates.
**D.J.Joe** Major accident in the kitchen.
**Marjory** If you would like to take a drink and stay here you might have a minute to yourselves, before the other guests arrive. D.J. - leave the tray, I'd like a word.
**D.J.Joe** Well, that's an odd couple. So? ... ...What do you want?
**Marjory** Nothing.
**D.J.Joe** Nothing? What did you call me out for then?
**Marjory** Give them a minute.
**D.J.Joe** Oh, right. .... Say ... What did happen in the kitchen?
**Marjory** Not now!

> *D.J.Joe peeps through at the couple. Marjory puts on her cardigan. D.J.Joe puts on his black tie*

**Nesta** *(in the Gazebo)* Of course to begin with we didn't think she'd last long. I'd go round, bring her the odd bit of shopping, sit with her. But ... she became more and more demanding. It reached the point where I couldn't cope any more. I had my own life - my work in the filing department, we were being computerised.

> *The music reaches a crescendo and stops*

Then I wasn't going to miss my place on the rota for the Age Concern shop.

We had a chat, didn't we Dolly? That you must pull your weight. So, since you were at home all day, except for that little part time job of yours at the Post Office, you were able to take over. She, Aunt Polly, God rest her, enjoyed seeing you, Tracy and Alexander, every morning before school, each afternoon on the way home, before Dolly went home to make your tea Arthur. So it worked very well, very well indeed.
Where are they with the food? *(helps herself to another sherry)* We've been waiting hours. *(calls)* Excuse me ... Excuse me...

> *Black tie in place, black cardigan on, Marjory and D.J.Joe*
> *collect trays of food, and take them through. In his effort to*
> *please D.J.Joe attempts silver service with the sandwiches.*
> *Both have serious voices and faces*

**Marjory** Right! In with the sandwiches and scones. I'll do the teas and coffee.

> *Takes in items, leaves them*

**D.J.Joe** Right! Madame, what can I tempt you to? Tuna? Ham? Egg mayonnaise? ... or perhaps a scone?

> *D.J.Joe notices there's no music*

**Nesta** One egg, one ham.

> *D.J.Joe makes a mess of silver service. Nesta waves him to*
> *put the plate down. Marjory is making signals from the door*

**Marjory** Quicker! The wedding guests are coming! This lots got all they are getting. Late anyway.
**D.J.Joe** They've no music in there. Just six chatting will be awful with no music.
**Marjory** One person spouting off you mean. Should have checked it properly. Too late now, there might be time later.
**D.J.Joe** Where are they then?
**Marjory** Just coming.

> *They both go to look in at the bride and groom, changing ties*
> *and removing cardigan. The Man moves from the kitchen into*
> *the funeral, unseen by D.J.Joe*

**D.J.Joe** Dumpy little thing.
**Marjory** Is a bit, must be the way he likes them.
**D.J.Joe** How old?
**Marjory** Thirty five'ish.

**D.J.Joe** He must be really old, fifty at least?
**Marjory** *(defensive)* Good looking though.
**D.J.Joe** Yes, I suppose so.... I thought all brides were beautiful.
**Marjory** That's stupid!
**D.J.Joe** She's not, she's plain. Dumpy and plain. *(peeps)* They are not doing anything.
**Marjory** What did you expect them to be doing – throwing aside the crockery and having a quick one on the top table?
**D.J.Joe** MARJORY !!
**Marjory** Well! *(peeps)* See what you mean. He seems to be describing the room to her!
**D.J.Joe** Not even holding hands.
**Marjory** Here's more coming now. To starting positions.

*Both gather up trays of drinks. Nesta is still going strong*

**Nesta** Arthur, no, how could you say that?! I'd looked after Mother after Father went and Aunt Polly just thought I'd take her on next, since I was used to it. I had done my bit! Your children were at school, it was Dolly's turn. Really Arthur, how could you.

*Completely taking offence, she leaves to plump herself in a chair in the main reception area. She distracts D.J.Joe by ordering another sherry which he tries to serve while covering his red bow tie.*

*A tall elegant woman of about forty five comes in, seems uncertain. D.J.Joe is confused over his tie. Marjory signals D.J.Joe to go back to the wedding and comes forward to speak to the woman*

**Marjory** Good afternoon. Can I help you?
**Valerie** Can you direct me to the bar? There was no one on Reception.
**Marjory** Certainly Madame, it's over there. Drat, that means Angela's gone.

*Valerie ignores this information, goes to peer through 'The Orangery' door*

**Valerie** Thank you. What lovely curtains.
**Marjory** Was there something else?
**Valerie** No, thank you.
**Marjory** A drink perhaps, Madame?
**Valerie** No, thank you. *(obviously very uncomfortable)* I can just sit here, can't I?

**Marjory**  Yes, of course, Madame.

**Valerie**  Lovely curtains.

**Marjory**  Yes, thank you.

**Valerie**  Did you choose them?

**Marjory**  No, my daughter.

**Valerie**  I've a daughter.

**Marjory**  Really.

**Valerie**  Rachael. Lives with me. And a son. Simon. He's at college.

**Marjory**  Oh?

**Valerie**  Doing Engineering.

**Marjory**  Really.

**Valerie**  I like the chairs.

**Marjory**  Thank you Madame

**Valerie**  I wonder... where did you get them from?

**Marjory**  Smith and Plumpstead, I think.

**Valerie**  Very nice.

**Marjory**  Are you sure you don't want anything from the bar Madame?

**Valerie**  Quite sure, thank you.

**Marjory**  Well, if you'll excuse me, Let me know if there is anything you need.

**Valerie**  Perhaps...

**Marjory**  Was there something else?

**Valerie**  The ... The Appleyard wedding?

**Marjory**  Oh! You've come to the wedding! Most of the guests have arrived, but you haven't missed much. If you'd like to follow me...

**Valerie**  No, No ... It's alright thank you. *(peers, careful not to be seen from inside)*

**Marjory**  Eh ... Friends or relations?

**Valerie**  Neither.

**Marjory**  Oh? You don't recognise anyone?

**Valerie**  Yes, I mean, no. ... My ex-husband.

**Marjory**  Oh, I see. Does he expect you?

**Valerie**  Oh, yes. I'm invited.

**Marjory**  Very brave of you.

> *Marjory has to get on serving the wedding, so leaves Valerie nervously looking through the door. Nesta is in her own thoughts, but speaks as if to The Man who has followed her out and sits, ignoring her, studying his notes*

**Nesta**  Should be quite a bit of money ... from Aunt Polly. And only three of us to split it between. I doubt if Uncle George will get much, they never saw eye to eye, and he's quite comfortable in that sheltered housing of his, doesn't need it. So it should be half to Dolly, half to me.

*Satisfied with her calculations she returns to 'The Gazebo'. Valerie catches Marjory's eye. Marjory and D.J.Joe swop drinks trays*

**Marjory** All right?
**Valerie** Yes. Steve and Kath are there. There was no one else to do it you see.
**Marjory** Sorry?
**Valerie** Well, he asked Steve and he couldn't very well say no, could he?
**Marjory** No?
**Valerie** No. Be Best Man.
**Marjory** Oh, I see.
**Valerie** Put on the spot really. It all happened very quickly.
**Marjory** Oh.

*She tries to escape, taking food out of the wedding. Valerie hardly notices. The Man looks up at her every so often while he takes notes of the lounge*

**Valerie** On one of my weekly trips to see that the house was O.K. he produced this questionnaire. All very organised. Said he was off to meet someone on Friday and what did I think. Well, what are you supposed to say when your husband says he's off to order a wife? That's what it amounts to, he put in an order for her. I'd to meet her, yes.
I got an invitation. When I got there she was at the sink. Pleasant girl ... well hardly a girl, but you know what I mean. Should suit him. He needs to be looked after, and she'll do that. Brought up to it, she said. Doesn't know anyone, none of our friends.

*Valerie looks through the door. The Man rises and looks through too, before going off to reception*

**Valerie** There's Steve and Kath, then our Simon and Rachael but no one else ... just office people. She will look after the house though. I'll not be needed there any more, thank goodness. My own little flat is very nice. A little sparse perhaps, but what I've got is good.

*Time is wearing on, Marjory and D.J.Joe need to prepare for the second funeral, but are caught by Valerie*

**Valerie** This carpet is nice.
**Marjory** Smith and Plumpstead.
**Valerie** Oh.
**Marjory** Are you all right Madame?

**Valerie**  Perhaps I will have a drink.
**Marjory**  Of course ....?
**Valerie**  Gin and tonic, please. That's lovely.

*Marjory serves her then looks in on Nesta*

**Marjory**  Get her out of there.*(putting on cardigan)*
**D.J.Joe**  Don't know why they are sitting there anyway. *(puts on black tie)*.
**Marjory**  If she doesn't want to go home, move her through here.
**D.J.Joe**  Excuse me... I'd like to clear...

> *D.J.Joe clears, trying to make her feel uncomfortable but
> she leans back to let him work round her*

**D.J.Joe**  She's not going to move.

*Marjory acts firmly*

**Marjory**  I'm sorry to disturb you but we do have another funeral to prepare for.
If you'd like to move through to the lounge again I'm sure you'd be very
comfortable.
**Nesta**  How awful to be rushed like this. I don't know if I will be able to think in
the lounge, all that coming and going. But if you insist...

> *Nesta moves to the lounge. D.J.Joe encourages her. As soon
> as she is out of the room D.J.Joe and Marjory clear the tables
> rapidly*

**D.J.Joe**  How many?
**Marjory**  *(refers to list)* Mr Ferguson - thirty.
**D.J.Joe**  Right. That doesn't need too much. Clear the wedding. Red tie.
**Marjory**  I'll check for crumbs.

> *Marjory goes of for the dust pan which she uses. D.J.Joe
> is caught in mid tie change. An older gentleman wanders in
> looking lost, clutching his cap. He is obviously upset. They use
> raised voices as though Sidney was deaf.*

**D.J.Joe**  The Ferguson funeral?
**Sidney**  No, not Ferguson - it was Jim Taylor.
**D.J.Joe**  Jim Taylor? Well, don't know who that would be then. It's Ferguson
we've got in here.
**Sidney**  I'm Ferguson.
**D.J.Joe**  Are you?!

**Sidney** I'd to arrange it,you see.
**D.J.Joe** So you made the booking?
**Sidney** Yes.
**D.J.Joe** Right then, come along.
**Sidney** I used to work here you see, part time like, but then I retired.
**D.J.Joe** Did you? Before my time then.

> *Marjory backs out with the dust pan into Sidney, engrossed in what she is doing*

**Marjory** Whoops, sorry. Just tidying up. *(takes dust pan away)*.
**Sidney** Marj? Marjory   ?
**Marjory** Yes, that's me. Sidney! *(they have a big, excited, cuddle.)* Sidney Ferguson! How are you? You are looking well. Let me go, you idiot! Lovely to see you! How is Ann?
**Sidney** She passed away two years ago.
**Marjory** Oh, dear, I am sorry to hear that. Oh, I am sorry.
**Sidney** Mmm, still miss her of course.
**Marjory** Of course. I saw the name Ferguson, never connected it with you.
**Sidney** No, lots of Ferguson's I suppose.
**Marjory** Yes.
**D.J.Joe** So who's died?
**Marjory** D.J.!
**Sidney** Jim Taylor.
**D.J.Joe** I know, but who's he then?
**Marjory** D.J.!

> *Marjory takes off cardigan, carries food to the wedding*

**Sidney** Used to sit with us on the seat outside the bank.
**D.J.Joe** So that's why I recognise you!
**Sidney** You're 'Nifty Shirts'.
**D.J.Joe** That's right!
**Sidney** Sandwiches from Simpson's every lunch time except Fridays when you go to The Crown.
**D.J.Joe** That's right! So which one's Jim Taylor? Not the tall thin one with the stick?
**Sidney** No, that's David.
**D.J.Joe** Oh, he always looks as if he is about to fall over.
**Sidney** He does.
**D.J.Joe** Does he?
**Sidney** Quite often really.
**D.J.Joe** Really? Never see it happen.

**Sidney**  Oh, quite often. Had to watch him at the cemetery. Nearly went but I
       caught him.
**D.J.Joe**  Not him then?
**Sidney**  No. Jim Taylor.
**D.J.Joe**  Jim Taylor.

*The Man wanders through to the wedding. Sidney looks at The
Man then enquiringly at D.J.Joe who shrugs, he doesn't know
who he is and they carry on*

**Sidney**  Always sat at the end near the bank door. Little fellow.
**D.J.Joe**  Oh him! Not him?!
**Sidney**  Yes. *(sad)*
**D.J.Joe**  Oh dear.
**Sidney**  Yes. *(very sad)*
**D.J.Joe**  Oh, I am sorry.
**Sidney**  Yes. *(near to tears)*
**D.J.Joe**  The kids will miss him.
**Sidney**  Yes. But he'd to stop doing it you know. *(swallows hard)*
**D.J.Joe**  What?
**Sidney**  Giving out the sweets?
**D.J.Joe**  Really?
**Sidney**  Ester Ranzen's fault of course.
**D.J.Joe**  Oh...?
**Sidney**  Kids wouldn't talk to strange men, upset him at first, until he found the
       dogs.
**D.J.Joe**  The dogs... Yes.

*Marjory has been serving and clearing. She puts her cardigan
on. D.J.Joe moves to the funeral to set up*

**Marjory**  Excuse me but there is quite a crowd coming in by the back door.
**Sidney**  Marjory? ...
**Marjory**  Sidney. *(cuddle)*
**Sidney**  Don't see you go past the bank.
**Marjory**  I don't live here now.
**Sidney**  Oh. I know.
**Marjory**  No, just came in to let my daughter away for a couple of days.
**Sidney**  Now would that be Kim or Rosemary?
**Marjory**  Rosemary! She's manager.
**Sidney**  Rosemary is?
**Marjory**  Yes. How do you remember their names?!
**Sidney**  Good with names, always have been. And Bill?

**Marjory** He's fine too. Look, Sid, I'm sorry to rush you, but we've a wedding
on too. The rest of your party are through there.
**Sidney** So how many hotels have you got now?
**Marjory** Shh! Sid.
**Sidney** Why? You should be proud of yourselves!
**Marjory** D.J. doesn't know Bill and I own it.
**Sidney** Alright, .... Why?
**Marjory** Sid!
**Sidney** Of course, of course... through here?
**Marjory** Yes. I'll try and catch up with you later.

*Sidney moves through to the funeral. The Man comes from the
wedding carrying a handful of cruet sets*

**Marjory** Do you have to do that now? It's not certain you know. They are
discussing it now, my husband and daughter. Five o'clock our letter said.

*The Man shrugs and moves to reception*

**D.J.Joe** Who was that?
**Marjory** Not now.

*Marjory gives a big sigh that warns D.J.Joe not to ask*

**D.J.Joe** O.K. then... I'll do these funeral drinks will I? I've still got the right tie on.
**Marjory** Right. I think I'll come in with you to make sure everyone is happy.

*Marjory checks the black cardigan and follows D.J.Joe. We hear
them both chatting to the local people D.J.Joe sees every day,
and people Marjory hasn't seen for ages. D.J.Joe is cheery, but
changes to sad*

**D.J.Joe** Hallo, Mrs Smith how are you today? ... Oh, I'm sorry, not thinking.
Would you like a paper napkin? There. Blow. That's better. Sherry?
No? Orange. Here we are then. That should buck you up a bit...I
think...
**Marjory** Mr Dodds how are you? Sad occasion. Poor Mr Taylor. I'm doing fine
thank you. No, we don't come back often enough. Bill was saying to
give best wishes to anyone who remembers him. Yes. If you will excuse
me now... Mrs Smith. Mrs Bates and Mrs Chater, well, well ... Mr Chater,
Mr Manners nice to see you even on such a sad occasion, yes...

*Marjory escapes to order more food and find more plates.
D.J.Joe calls Sidney out*

**D.J.Joe** How did he die? It all seems very sudden.
**Sidney** A Rotwheiller.
**D.J.Joe** Oh. No!
**Sidney** Yes.
**D.J.Joe** Badly injured?
**Sidney** No, not a mark on him.
**D.J.Joe** ... ...the Rotwheiller?
**Sidney** No, Jim.
**D.J.Joe** So...?
**Sidney** It was the sweets you see. Jim got friendly with all the dogs. This Rotwheiller loved him, they all did ...*(near to tears)* We all did. Tried to get into his pocket - for the sweets you see. Knocked him over, owner couldn't pull him off. There he was, sitting on top of him, licking him.
**D.J.Joe** Jim Taylor?
**Sidney** No, the Rotwheiller. Had to give him all the sweets before we could get him off. Took him into the bank but he'd gone.
**D.J.Joe** Just like that.
**Sidney** Yes. The owner wanted to bring him, the dog, to the funeral but we advised her against it.
**D.J.Joe** Very wise.

> *They go back to the company. Marjory checks on events in the wedding. Valerie is sitting in a position where she can see into the wedding but not be seen by them. Nesta is searching in her bag for paper and pen, fails to find any*

**Nesta** Do you have any paper?
**Marjory** If you would like to ask at reception I'm sure Angela would be able to find you some. Oh no, Angela's left, look behind the counter. *(takes off cardigan)*
**Nesta** Thank you.

> Nesta *goes off*

**Marjory** *(to Valerie after going to check that all is  well in the wedding reception)* Are you all right?
**Valerie** Yes, I think so. Is it all going well through there? He did so want it to go well. Asked me out to coffee, to discuss the arrangements, would you believe. It wasn't the arrangements at all. Well, it might have been at the beginning. 'You are a very attractive woman, Val', he said. Well, I know that, you do know, don't you? If you are attractive or not? 'It's a bit late to notice that now', I said, 'You are getting married next week'. 'We should never have split up, you know'. Oh, yes we should. The bruises. He did

them, then forgot them. I'd to go round with them, feeling them, feeling people looking at me and doubting my excuses. The kids, they told me to go. If it hadn't been for them... they told me. 'Go', they said, 'Don't stay with the bugger, leave'.

**Marjory** So you did. Good for you, Madame. Good for you being here too. I don't know if I could have come.

**Valerie** 'United front', the kids said,' You come. We'll show him'.

**Marjory** Just you sit here. I'll get you something - another drink, coffee? *(puts on cardigan)*

**Valerie** I can't face going through.

**Marjory** I know. You can stay here as long as you like

> *Goes for coffee, returns with it. During the conversation, Nesta has returned with her paper and pen, but has been eaves dropping*

**Nesta** A man packing cruets gave me some.

**Marjory** Here. If you will excuse me...

> *Marjory leaves to serve tea and coffee to the funeral*

**Nesta** I couldn't help over hearing. Is that your ex-husband's wedding in there?

**Valerie** Yes.

**Nesta** Well, fancy that.

**Valerie** What?

**Nesta** You coming to his wedding.

**Valerie** I was invited, so of course I came.

**Nesta** Of course it would never have happened in my day.

**Valerie** What?

**Nesta** Wives going to ex-husband's weddings.

**Valerie** Why not? It's very civilised.

**Nesta** Why did he leave you? That the other woman?

**Valerie** No. And I left him.

**Nesta** Why?

**Valerie** If you must know ... he hit me.

**Nesta** Why?

**Valerie** I'm not really sure.

**Nesta** So what are you doing at his wedding?

**Valerie** He asked me.

**Nesta** And so you came.

**Valerie** Everyone in a divorce is very civilised now.

**Nesta** But he used to hit you!

**Valerie** Yes. If you'll excuse me.

*Valerie goes to the toilets, sobbing*

**Nesta**  Most odd.

> *Returns to her calculations, Marjory and D.J.Joe come and go, taking more plates of sandwiches and cake, and drinks into the funeral. D.J.Joe is singing the tunes from the wedding room. Marjory takes her cardigan off and takes drinks through to the wedding. The Man goes through to the toilets, clip board back in hand. Marjory gives him a threatening hiss*

**Nesta**  The house must be worth at least one hundred and twenty thousand, then she'd stocks. Say two hundred thousand in all, split three ways – Uncle George, Dolly and me. That's three in to twenty...let's say twenty one ... that's seven each, doesn't seem much... no! seventy! That's better, seventy. Where's the paper? *(finds a paper, turns pages until she finds story of competition winner)* Right, these pensioners..., pensioners, what a waste, won two hundred and four thousand, it says if they invest it they could get income of twenty thousand a year. So... my seventy could bring in about seven, a bit less, maybe. About seven thousand a year.

> *Marjory comes through from the wedding looking for Valerie goes on to the toilets and comes back with Valerie. Marjory turns the music down*

**Marjory**  They are just about to do the toast, I thought you might ...
**Valerie**  Yes, yes I will...
**Marjory**  I'll come with you. Here's a glass.

*They move to the entrance to the wedding*

**Valerie**  Thank you. *(tries to back out of the doorway, but Marjory pushes her forward)*
**Marjory**  No. Stand here. I'm right behind you.
**Valerie**  Oh, John and Pauline ... once it was John and Valerie...
**Marjory**  Hold on Madame.
**Valerie**  Oh, I can't...
**Marjory**  You beat her any day.
**Valerie**  *(preening a little, but still ready to cry)* Thank you.
**Marjory**  The Bride and Groom, go on!
**Valerie**  *(quietly)* The Bride and Groom.
**Marjory**  They never heard you.
**Valerie**  *(too loudly)* The Bride and Groom.

**Marjory**  Well done!
**Nesta**  Most odd!

*Marjory and Valerie come back elated*

**Nesta**  Most odd.
**Marjory**  Not at all.
**Valerie**  I did it! And I meant it! Did you see their faces?!
**Marjory**  Well done.
**Valerie**  *(looking down trying not to cry)* Lovely carpet.
**Marjory**  Smith and Plumpstead.
**Valerie**  Of course. *(runs sobbing to the toilets)*

> *D.J.Joe comes from the funeral with a huge smile on his face,*
> *but he tries to wipe it off to appear aggrieved*

**D.J.Joe**  Where have you been? I've just about done the whole of this funeral
myself. There are more than thirty you know ...
**Marjory**  More like fifty, I know. I did put out the extra plates for you. And got
the chef to do more sandwiches...
**D.J.Joe**  All ham...
**Marjory**  He'd thought he'd finished. Bloody lucky he did it at all!
**D.J.Joe**  Well... You just left me to it.
**Valerie**  *(coming from the toilet)* There's a man in there counting toilet rolls.
**Marjory**  Ignore him.
**Valerie**  I did try, but he was telling me all the fittings came from Masons. Very
good plumbers, Masons. ... ... ... I'm sorry, you are busy.
**D.J.Joe**  Is that the same man who....
**Marjory**  Yes.
**D.J.Joe**  So what the hell...
**Marjory**  Not now! Look I have done just about every thing for the flipping
wedding. And you're having a whale of a time!

*D.J.Joe recovers his good humour*

**D.J.Joe**  Yeh! It's great through there! You should come. There's a load of kids
all eating sweets fit to burst! Sidney brought them. Said it's what Jim
would have wanted. And all the folk Jim and the old blokes speak to on the
bank corner. David has fallen over twice!
**Marjory**  I think I'll just leave you to it.
**D.J.Joe**  No, you should come in. The wedding food is finished, isn't it? Come on,
lots of people are asking about you, what you and ....er,Bill, are doing now.
I don't know do I? Come on.

**Marjory**  No, it's all right. You enjoy it.

**D.J.Joe**  And, you know what?! That old bloke from the other funeral he's in there too - telling jokes to the kids. They are loving it!

**Nesta**  Who?

**D.J.Joe**  Your friend.

**Nesta**  Uncle George?!

**D.J.Joe**  Yeh, that's what the kids were calling him!

**Nesta**  Well... But he's deaf!

**D.J.Joe**  Not him!

**Marjory**  Remember the disco.

**D.J.Joe**  In here? *(the funeral)*

**Marjory**  No! The Wedding!

**D.J.Joe**  But they're leaving. So ... in here?

**Marjory**  Oh, please yourself!

> *Marjory begins to clear the food from the wedding reception. She nods encouragement to Valerie who moves through. The Man comes from the toilets clutching a pile of toilet rolls. Marjory takes them off him*

**Marjory**  Get lost!

> *The Man stays in the lounge as Marjory puts the toilet rolls back in the toilet. He stays in the lounge annoying Marjory more and more, but she still has a hotel to run. Nesta is still studying her calculations*

**Marjory**  Is there anything I could get you?

**Nesta**  A cup of tea would be nice, thank you.

**Marjory**  Tea? Certainly. ...*(putting on cardigan and muttering under her breath)* Oh, we have an expert here! She'll get the cup have a good peer inside it to make sure it's clean. Tea. She knows the coffee will be stewed by now or we'll be onto instant. Tea it is. Oh dear, I must be getting tired. They don't usually get to me. But I'm not usually doing all this most of the time, just occasionally. Funerals. Always fat people at funerals. Fat ladies particularly. Wonder how they manage in that loo? There's no space. They must plop round that door like a balloon about to burst. And smoking! Everyone at funerals seems to smoke, weddings are not so bad, but funerals ... must all be rushing to join the dear departed by the only sure method they know. Tea. Tea, Madame.

**Nesta**  Thank you. *(looks into cup to make sure it's clean while Marjory watches).*

**Marjory**  *(to Valerie)* Tea, Madame?

**Valerie**  A gin and tonic please.

**Marjory** Of course.

*Serves tea. Sidney comes in looking for Marjory*

**Sidney** It's hectic in there! So, how are you Marjory?
**Marjory** Tired!
**Sidney** You are not used to this anymore, are you?
**Marjory** You could say that again.
**Sidney** You are not used to ....
**Marjory** Sidney!
**Sidney** Well, gone up in the world now, you and Bill, haven't you.
**Marjory** Well...
**Sidney** Pay people to do it now. You can tell me.
**Marjory** These walls have ears, Sidney.
**Sidney** Oh... Right, I understand. But I liked working here, you know.
**Marjory** I know, so did I.
**Sidney** You won't come back.
**Marjory** Only sometimes, like this.
**Sidney** I understand.

*Marjory draws Sidney away from The Man who may be listening*

**Marjory** And you Sid. Has it been awful since Ann died?
**Sidney** I've got used to it. Dab hand at the Sunday diner now. The boys still
come over for it, bring the children, little brats.
**Marjory** And their wives?
**Sidney** Fine girls, both of them. But they'd organise me given half a chance! I
manage fine on my own. Do my own bit of shopping in the morning, then
a chat with my mates at the bank. Bit of cleaning, bit of gardening, then
back to the bank again if it's fine.
**Marjory** You've a good crowd of mates there.
**Sidney** Yes, same lot I went to school with mostly. All put out of the house so
that their wives can get on with the house work and have their friends
round for coffee. The wives take it hard, retirement.
**Marjory** Bill and I are used to being together the whole time so it shouldn't
bother us when the time comes.
**Sidney** Got plans have you?
**Marjory** We were planning to retire to the Scilly Isles.
**Sidney** You must have made quite a pile by now.
**Marjory** Mmm...
**Sidney** Quite a team, you and Bill.
**Marjory** Yes.
**Sidney** Remember the Bed and Breakfast in Malvern Road?

**Marjory**  Yes.
**Sidney**  That's where I first met you.
**Marjory**  Helped me out with the rubbish bags. You lived at number thirty six.
**Sidney**  Bill was still working then.
**Marjory**  Always gave a hand with the breakfasts before he left though.
**Sidney**  I bet you end up doing bed and breakfast in the Scilly Isles! You'll not be able to stop yourselves!
**Marjory**  Maybe not the Scilly Isles.
**Sidney**  Lots of ideas have you?
**Marjory**  Well...
**Sidney**  Secretive as ever, eh? Marjory? Never know what you and Bill would move on to next.

*Sidney looks back to the funeral*

**Sidney**  That George is a nice bloke.
**Marjory**  Who?
**Sidney**  George - didn't know if he was going to make it to Jim's because his sister died the same week. And here he is, in the same hotel, the funeral before Jim's. That's two people he'll miss, all in one week. Used to visit his sister regular, lonely old soul, she was, by all accounts, on her own  in that big house. Well, someone will get that I suppose. George doesn't need it.

*Nesta coughs, which attracts Sidney attention*

**Sidney**  *(to Nesta)* You were at George's sister's funeral weren't you? You work at the Age Concern shop on the High Street don't you? Seen you there.
**Nesta**  Sometimes, yes.
**Sidney**  Quite regular I would  have  said,  see  you  most days.
**Nesta**  Not every day, I work.
**Sidney**  Benson's.
**Nesta**  That's right.
**Sidney**  Lot of changes there.
**Nesta**  Some, yes.
**Sidney**  Didn't affect you then?
**Nesta**  A little.
**Sidney**  Oh..?
**Nesta**  A little.
**Sidney**  Just a little?
**Nesta**  Yes.
**Sidney**  Nice day for it?
**Nesta**  What?

**Sidney** A funeral.
**Nesta** Oh.
**Sidney** Great crowd through there, you know. You should come through.
*(to Valerie)* You are very quiet. Do you want to come through?

*Valerie gets to her feet*

**Nesta** Thank you but no.
**Sidney** Suit yourself, you've been asked.
**Nesta** Thank you.
**Sidney** Right then, I'll go  back. Come on then, young lady. *(leads Valerie)*
**Nesta** Yes.
**Sidney** I'll speak to you next time.
**Nesta** Next time?
**Sidney** Next time I see you going to the Age Concern shop.
**Nesta** Oh, yes.
**Sidney** Do you dance?
**Valerie** Quite well actually!

*Nesta sits staring into space. Sidney back to the funeral.*
*Marjory calls D.J.Joe from the funeral*

**Marjory** D.J. We are going to have to get a move on.
**D.J.Joe** Right. Yes. Sorry. Enjoying myself. There's an old bloke through there,
married he is, telling me about this affair he's having...
**Marjory** D. J. You've a disco to do.

*The Man is still looking blandly, like wallpaper. Marjory is edgy*
*with D.J.Joe and he's had enough*

**D.J.Joe** Who is that?
**Marjory** Who?
**D.J.Joe** Him!
**Marjory** Oh, him. He's waiting.
**D.J.Joe** Then why the hell isn't he working?
**Marjory** Not that kind of waiter. He's waiting.
**D.J.Joe** What for?
**Marjory** To clear.
**D.J.Joe** Well he could start on....
**Marjory** No, No. Just ignore him, .....do the disco!
**D.J.Joe** But... oh, alright if you say so.

*Sidney comes back*

**Sidney**  Where's this disco then?

**D.J.Joe**  Don't you start.

**Sidney**  Hey! What do you mean?

**D.J.Joe**  It's her. Giving me a hard time. Because of that bloke.

**Sidney**  Who?

**D.J.Joe**  Him!

**Sidney**  Good afternoon. *(The Man nods)* Seems O.K. From the wedding is he?

**Marjory**  Do the disco D.J.

**D.J.Joe**  Alright, I'm going, but what's got into you all of a sudden?

**Marjory**  D.J.!

**D.J.Joe**  O.K.,O.K.

*D.J.Joe leaves for the funeral*

**Sidney**  Well?

**Marjory**  Well what?

**Sidney**  You never get rattled.

**Marjory**  Well, I am now. *(to The Man)* Excuse me, haven't you got something to do? More lists to make up? More cruets to collect?

*The Man moves to the kitchen*

**Sidney**  So, he's working?

**Marjory**  You could call it that.

**Sidney**  What's he doing?

**Marjory**  Collecting cruets.

**Sidney**  And you are letting him collect yours?!

**Marjory**  I can't stop him.

**Sidney**  Of course you can, I'll stop him for you.

**Marjory**  Leave it Sid.

**Sidney**  Don't be bloody daft woman! He'll start on the bar next.

**Marjory**  Probably.

**Sidney**  What?! And you'll let him, I suppose?!

**Marjory**  Nothing I can do about it.

**Sidney**  Oh yes there is!

**Marjory**  No Sid.

**Sidney**  What do you mean? Who the hell does he think he is?

**Marjory**  The Bailiff.

**Sidney**  What! Why?!

**Marjory**  He's done his lists, so now he'll start collecting what he wants.

**Sidney**  Over my dead body!

**Marjory**  Leave it, Sid!

**Sidney**  What happened?!
**Marjory**  We got a bit over-drawn, ...
**Sidney**  You've coped before!
**Marjory**  Not this time. Oh, hell. *(looks towards the different function rooms. looks at Nesta. Looks at The Man).* Oh, hell! I'm going up to Rosemary's room for five minutes. Tell D.J..
**Sidney**  *(giving her a quick cuddle)* You do that. I'll see about him. *(nods in the direction of The Man)*

> *Marjory hurries out. Sidney shouts for D.J.Joe the music is blaring*

**D.J.Joe**  What now? It's going great.
**Sidney**  Clear that wedding.
**D.J.Joe**  What! Don't you start. I've had it up to here with her!
**Sidney**  Clear that wedding. There's a spot of bother. That man is going to take the lot.
**D.J.Joe**  What lot.
**Sidney**  All the crockery, everything.
**D.J.Joe**  What's he want it for?
**Sidney**  To sell.
**D.J.Joe**  Of all the bloody nerve!!
**Sidney**  The Bailiff.
**D.J.Joe**  Bloody hell! O.K. You're on!! You done this before?
**Sidney**  You bet!
**D.J.Joe**  O.K. In reverse!
**Sidney**  Dirty napkins.
**D.J.Joe**  Dirty glasses.
**Sidney**  Coffee cups.
**D.J.Joe**  ...And fork...

> *A rushed version of the setting up sequence. Nesta is oblivious at first then watches in astonishment. The Man is removing furniture. The black out comes on D.J.Joe seeing Nesta standing holding out her cup, he grabs it. The stage is bare only Nesta is left*

> *Blackout. End of Act One*

## LILIES AND CARNATIONS.

## ACT TWO.

> *A bed sitting room/office belonging to Rosemary, Marjory's daughter and manager of the hotel. Marjory enters, shuts the door and leans against it*

**Marjory** Oh, hell! Hell, hell, hell! What a bloody mess. I tried, I really did try.

> *Marjory moves to look out of the window, staring into space, trying to gather her thoughts*

God, it's cold in here. Oh, Bill, Rosemary, I did try. That bloody Bailiff. Snoop, snoop, snoop. Kept getting in my way, reminding me.

> *Cuddles herself in cold and depression*

How could I stay calm for the guests with him popping up all over the place. ... Guests. Pain in the backside, all of them ... except Sid of course.

> *Marjory looks around the room*

Very neat, tidy. ... That old hag counting her money..... And that woman on about the furniture.

> *Marjory looks at room in more detail*

So tidy! You were never like this a home Rosemary!

> *Marjory can't resist a look at the pile of books and papers on the desk*

Accounts, Bookings, Running Bills – very organised. Old Register, Bar receipts. I'll look at them properly ...tomorrow if we're lucky.

> *It is cold, she shivers. she stares into space, gradually coming back to reality*

'Put the fire on', she said, 'It may look old but it works'. Good.

> *Marjory flicks the switch. goes to her bag for a handkerchief and*

*finds a box of matches*

Palace Hotel - huh!

*Marjory blows her nose looks at the desk again, rubs her hands together. She goes back to the desk then to the fire which is dead*

Hum...

*Marjory clicks the switch again and looks for the colour then uses her hand to feel for any warmth. There is none. She lifts the fire looks at it then follows the cable under the desk. She leans across the desk to try to reach, knocking papers onto the floor. She comes up for air and to assess. She goes under the desk but things block the end of the cable. She attempts to move the desk into the middle of the room. She finds the plug and is delighted. Holds it and looks round for the socket. It is not obvious so she puts the fire on the desk and goes in search of the socket. She finds the socket and goes back for the plug. She walks with the plug as far as it will go - which is no where near the socket. She lifts the fire, plugs it in and stretches it as far as it will go into the room. She switches it on, checks, and it works. She appreciates it's warmth before going back to look at the desk, starts to tidy it*

**Marjory** Accounts, Bar receipts ... no, .... accounts, old register, bookings .... Oh, God! I can't remember how they were. Now she'll think I've been prying. Let's just....

*Marjory takes a pile of papers to the chair and sits to go though them*

It should never have happened.

*She's cold. Attempts to move the chair nearer the fire by it's arms, with the papers on her knee. They all slide off onto the floor. She sits back staring at the ceiling*

**Marjory** Oh hell, ohhh! (*she sits huddled close to the fire*) Funerals and weddings...

*Marjory shuts her eyes and sighs. There is a gentle knocking at the door*

**Marjory** Go away.
**Sidney** It's me. Sid.
**Marjory** Go away Sid.
**Sidney** No.
**Marjory** Leave me alone for a bit, Sid. I'll be alright in a few minutes then I'll
come down.
**Sidney** No. Let me in.
**Marjory** Sid, please.
**Sidney** Come on young lady. We've things to do.

> *Marjory goes to open the door, then goes back to sit on the
> chair*

**Marjory** There.

> *Sidney lifts a box of heavy dishes and staggers in*

**Sidney** Where do you want them?
**Marjory** What the....?
**Sidney** Well, he's not getting them.
**Marjory** *(clears a space on the desk)* Put them anywhere.
**Sidney** There's more.

> *D.J.Joe follows in with another box*

**Sidney** Right lad. Down there.
**D.J.Joe** Right Sid. Next lot?
**Sidney** Yes, off you go son.

> *D.J.Joe leaves. Sid sits, puffed out on the desk beside Marjory*

Oh, not as fit as I thought. God, it's hot in here. *(turns fire off)*

**Marjory** Don't know why you're bothering Sid. They are going to take it all
anyway.
**Sidney** Over my dead body!
**Marjory** It's nothing to do with you Sid. It's me and Bill and Rosemary that are
going to loose the lot.
**Sidney** You gave me the barman job when me and Ann were pretty desperate.
I owe you.
**Marjory** That was years ago, silly old bugger. *(Gives him a hug)* Go back to
your funeral.
**Sidney** Can't.

**Marjory**  Why not? It was going so well.
**Sidney**  They've all gone to George's.
**Marjory**  But...
**Sidney**  That Bailiff fellow tried to take the sweets off the kids. Set them all off crying.
**Marjory**  Oh no!
**Sidney**  My pals couldn't have that. Not with Jim being so fond of the kids, and it being his funeral and that, so...
**Marjory**  So they've gone.
**Sidney**  George led them off in a crocodile down the street to the Anchor.

*D.J.Joe staggers in with another box*

**D.J.Joe**  Where do you want it?
**Marjory**  Anywhere.
**Sidney**  Now, come on pull yourself together.
**D.J.Joe**  I still don't understand.
**Sidney**  They are going to take the lot.
**D.J.Joe**  What everything?
**Sidney**  Everything that can be moved.
**D.J.Joe**  God!
**Sidney**  Yes.
**D.J.Joe**  Bloody hell! My disco!! *(he runs off)*
**Sidney**  Thought that would make him move!

*They both smile. Pause*

So how long has this been brewing, Marj?
**Marjory**  Three weeks or so.
**Sidney**  Couldn't you do anything?
**Marjory**  Just hope it wouldn't happen. Keep the business going. Carry on as normal. The staff have all been sacked you know.
**Sidney**  Oh dear.
**Marjory**  Yes.

*Pause*

**Sidney**  Does your Dad know?
**Marjory**  God forbid!
**Sidney**  *(laughs)* God forbid!
**Marjory**  Let's hope he does, eh, Sid?!
**Sidney**  Yes. He'd not be pleased.
**Marjory**  No.

**Sidney**  How is the old fellow.
**Marjory**  Mmm. So-so.
**Sidney**  Still at the same home?
**Marjory**  'Vicar's Retreat', yes.
**Sidney**  Bloody silly name.
**Marjory**  Appropriate.
**Sidney**  Yes, of course.
**Marjory**  If he found out...
**Sidney**  Then one vicar told another vicar that your vicar's...
**Marjory**  ... daughter has had the bailiffs in.

*It has become a joke, but then serious*

... I don't know what it would do to him.

*Both sit and stare into space, before coming back to the matter in hand. Marjory is just about ready to cope again*

**Sidney**  Boxes. We could do with more boxes. Have you got any?
**Marjory**  There's a cupboard off the kitchen.
**Sidney**  Right.
**Marjory**  It's locked. *(finds large bunch of keys)* Here.

*Sidney goes off. Marjory looks at the boxes and starts to rearrange them. There is a knock and the door opens straight away)*

**Nesta**  Ah, here you are.
**Marjory**  Miss... What do YOU want?
**Nesta**  I thought I'd like to pay the bill for Aunt Polly.
**Marjory**  It doesn't matter.
**Nesta**  Oh yes, I like to keep up to date with these things. I couldn't find the woman on reception so I thought I'd look for you as you seemed to be in charge.
**Marjory**  *(looking at the chaos of the desk)* It's not written out yet.
**Nesta**  Well, would you do it now please. And remember the reduction for the cups.
**Marjory**  I'll send it to you.
**Nesta**  I would rather do it now. I'm like that. No bills, no debts, no worries.
**Marjory**  Huh!
**Nesta**  Sorry? I beg your pardon?
**Marjory**  Nothing. I don't know what it comes to.
**Nesta**  Well, I can tell you. Tea for six.

**Marjory**  You booked for thirty.

**Nesta**  Yes, well... but we only had six.

**Marjory**  I should charge you for thirty. You certainly had more than six sherries.

**Nesta**  But only six people. And if you are going to be awkward, I'd like to object to the paper cups and the marmalade. Aunt Polly hated it.

**Marjory**  Your Aunt Polly wasn't there!

**Nesta**  But she would have if she had been. And it was her day.

**Marjory**  God!

**Nesta**  I'd prefer it if you didn't swear.

**Marjory**  *(sighs, gives in)* Alright, your bill.

> She searches though the chaos of the desk, finds a scrappy
> piece of paper and writes it out. Nesta looks at the paper with
> disgust

**Nesta**  Thank you. And I really must say that I think your place is down stairs.

**Marjory**  Thank you.

**Nesta**  It's the children. Very upset. What a noise. Though why people take children to a funeral is beyond me.

**Marjory**  They were fond of the old gentleman who died. They do bury their hamsters and budgies.

**Nesta**  Well, may be. But all that crying.

**Marjory**  I understand they have left now.

**Nesta**  Yes, but then ... that man...

**Marjory**  I know about that man.

**Nesta**  But he's...

**Marjory**  I know.

**Nesta**  *(paying the bill)* Well, if you know about it All I can say is it's a very odd way to run a hotel - children running in and out, removal men, and on top of it all, marmalade. Would you sign this as paid.

**Marjory**  Of course. *(does so, and hands it back)*

**Nesta**  *(putting bill carefully into her bag)* Thank you. Now I can get off to the solicitors.

**Marjory**  For the reading of the will.

**Nesta**  Yes.

**Marjory**  See how much money you're going to get.

**Nesta**  Well!

**Marjory**  Money and a house wasn't it? Very nice when you were so fond of your aunt.

**Nesta**  I don't think...

**Marjory**  No, obviously.

**Nesta**  Oh, this is too much! This is the last time...

**Marjory**  Good!

Act 2

35

*Nesta leaves in a huff*

Oh, sod it!

*Sidney struggles in with another box*

**Sidney** Got rid of that one did you? Good! Mean cow. Right. Next lot.

*Sidney starts to leave but Marjory looks in the box*

**Marjory** What have you got there?!
**Sidney** The till. Empty.
**Marjory** Oh, Sid. *(begins to laugh)*
**Sidney** Well, it was the first thing of any value I came across. I've got that woman from the wedding helping now.

*D.J.Joe struggles in with disco gear*

**D.J.Joe** Can I leave this lot here while I bring the van round.
**Marjory** Of course.
**D.J.Joe** There's more. *(goes off)*
**Marjory** What are you going for next?
**Sidney** What do you want?
**Marjory** I could do with a drink.
**Sidney** Right. *(heads off straight away)*
**Marjory** No Sid! ...Too late.

*Valerie comes in half drunk and carrying display flowers, which she presents to Marjory.)*

**Valerie** Here!
**Marjory** What are these for?
**Valerie** The old man, Sidney isn't it? Said to take something to you. So I had a look round and thought this was probably the nicest thing.
**Marjory** Thank you.
**Valerie** That's alright. You've been very kind and helpful to me today. Least I could do.
**Marjory** Thank you.
**Valerie** This is a very interesting room. Oh! I like...

*She goes to touch some ornament*

**Marjory** *(snapping)* Don't touch!
**Valerie** I'm sorry.
**Marjory** No. I'm sorry. It's my daughter's you see.
**Valerie** *(embarrassed, looks round)* Right then. I'll go now.
**Marjory** The weddings finished?
**Valerie** No one there. Must have gone when I was at the funeral.
**Marjory** Oh.
**Valerie** Now I've had a good cry and a good dance I feel much better. Out to
    face the world, eh?
**Marjory** Yes.
**Valerie** Goodbye then. And thanks again.
**Marjory** Goodbye.

*She goes to leave but bumps into Nesta*

**Nesta** Where do you think you're going?
**Valerie** Well, I thought I'd drop into the Anchor, if it's any of your business.
**Nesta** No, you can't.
**Valerie** Hey, wait a minute! It's a wedding I've been not a bloody funeral like
    you.
**Nesta** Door's locked
**Valerie** I'll unlock it.
**Nesta** You can't
**Marjory** Why not?
**Nesta** There's police on guard. They won't let anyone in or out.
**Marjory** Oh no! Well, ... if you'd like to sit in the lounge, I'll try and sort this lot
    out.
**Valerie** We can't. No chairs.
**Nesta** They loaded them onto a lorry.
**Marjory** Oh. Sit here then while I go and see.
**D.J.Joe** *(with the rest of the disco gear)* Ah, Ladies. Right, I'm going for my van
**Nesta, Marjory, Valerie** You can't.
**D.J.Joe** Too many people telling what I can and can't do! As far as I can see
    there will be no more disco needed here today, so I'm off.
**Marjory** No, D.J.. They've locked us in.
**D.J.Joe** What?!

*Sidney comes in with a box of drink, with optics attached.*
*Marjory goes to help him. He whispers*

**Sidney** We're locked in.
**Nesta, Valerie, Marjory** We know.

*All goes quiet as they look at each other*

**D.J.Joe** What the hell is going on?
**Marjory** I need a drink.
**Valerie** What a good idea. *(she serves everyone)*

*Silence that Sidney eventually breaks*

**Sidney** Well ... that bloke ... he's the Bailiff.
**D.J.Joe** So you said. But what the....??
**Sidney** Marjory...?
**Marjory** He wouldn't wait. Kept on making his lists. Now they've loaded the first lot. Wouldn't wait until five o'clock, would he?
**Sidney** Why five o'clock?
**Marjory** They should know by then.
**Nesta** Who should know?
**Marjory** Bill and Rosemary.
**Valerie** Who?
**Sidney** *(aside)* Husband and daughter.
**Nesta** Rosemary ... she's the polite young lady who ... and you're her Mother, well, I'd never have thought...
**Valerie** Shh!
**Marjory** *(deep sigh)* We own this hotel, and the Palace, and the Anchor.
**Valerie** Oh, do you own the Anchor ... I was going...
**Nesta** Shh!
**D.J.Joe** Shouldn't bother. No chairs either, by now.
**Marjory** We hit a problem with cash flow.
**Nesta** You're in debt, you mean!
**Sidney** If Marjory says cash flow, she means cash flow.
**Marjory** We over spent on our food and wine account.
**D.J.Joe** So now they are taking it off you.
**Valerie** By taking the lovely furniture.
**Marjory** Yes, but...
**Nesta** Have we eaten food that's not paid for? I want my money back!
**D.J.Joe** Only six teas!
**Marjory** We've got half the money. But we got charged. False references they said, but it was nothing of the sort. They were all sound. The Court wouldn't wait. Bailiffs have writs on all the hotels in the group.
**D.J.Joe** So what's this about five o'clock?
**Marjory** They should be out of court by then.
**Valerie** Who?
**Marjory** Bill and Rosemary.
**Nesta** Criminals!

**Marjory**  They should get off.
**Nesta**  And if they don't?
**Marjory**  I'm not thinking about it.
**D.J.Joe**  So that Bailiff bloke is a bit quick off the mark, isn't he?
**Sidney**  Exactly!
**Valerie**  So you're guilty before proved innocent.
**Marjory**  Something like that.
**Nesta**  Well. I don't know.
**D.J.Joe**  So we're stuck here.
**Marjory**  Yes.

*Long pause while they take in what that means*

**Valerie**  I'm getting hungry. Far too nervous to eat anything at the wedding.
**Sidney**  Hmm. Planning. That's what we need. Planning.
**Valerie**  Food. That's what I need.
**Sidney**  Right then. You and I will see what's left in the kitchen. Marjory, you
    come and make lists of items to bring in here. D.J., clear you gear we are
    going to need the space. And you...*(looks at Nesta)*
**Nesta**  I'll just stay here.
**Sidney**  On guard, good idea!

*Marjory, Valerie and Sidney leave. D.J.Joe starts to move his
disco gear out of the centre of the floor. Nesta watches*

**Nesta**  How's business?
**D.J.Joe**  Sorry?
**Nesta**  How's business.
**D.J.Joe**  That's what I thought you said.
**Nesta**  'Nifty Shirts' on King Street isn't it?
**D.J.Joe**  Yes, that's right. Very good, thank you.
**Nesta**  I thought so.
**D.J.Joe**  Why?
**Nesta**  Nothing. My nephew had on one of you shirts.
**D.J.Joe**  Did he?
**Nesta**  At my Aunt's funeral. He's gone now.
**D.J.Joe**  Oh?
**Nesta**  Very nice.
**D.J.Joe**  Thank you.
**Nesta**  Busy shop.
**D.J.Joe**  Doing very nicely, yes.
**Nesta**  Thinking of expanding?
**D.J.Joe**  Well...

**Nesta** Well?

**D.J.Joe** Could be.

**Nesta** I might have some money.

**D.J.Joe** Oh?

**Nesta** That I could invest.

**D.J.Joe** In 'Nifty Shirts'?

**Nesta** Possibly. I'm considering investing in something.

**D.J.Joe** Really? *(getting going on the patter)* Well, 'Nifty Shirts' would be a sound investment. You see at the moment we have everything in the one shop, - everything from sport shirts, through office wear and 'trendy' to diner suit shirts. It's all a bit squashed.

**Nesta** I'd noticed. A bit of a jumble.

**D.J.Joe** Well, I'd hardly call it a jumble.

**Nesta** The shop next door has been empty for some time.

**D.J.Joe** I know. It would be perfect. Expand into there.

**Nesta** I might be able to help.

**D.J.Joe** Really?

**Nesta** I'd need a return on my money of course.

**D.J.Joe** Of course.

**Nesta** And income, regular share of the profits.

**D.J.Joe** I understand.

**Nesta** If you had say seventy thousand...

**D.J.Joe** What? Seventy thousand?! What couldn't I do with seventy thousand! Two shops, linked with a through arch. Bright lighting in the sports section with pop music then as you moved through to 'trendys' and on to diner shirts, more of the pop classics perhaps. Old favourites in the office section. Decor is important of course. Costs a lot to get it right. But necessary, to bring them in off the street and keep them there. Once in they usually buy something, a tie at least. We've got a good range of ties ... ... Why me?

**Nesta** I need income ... from my capital. You seem to be a go ahead sort of young man.

**D.J.Joe** Oh, I am. Definitely.

**Nesta** Well then, we'll talk about it again shall we.

**D.J.Joe** Yes. Definitely.

**Nesta** Now, if you'll excuse me.

*She makes to go out having to climb over obstacles on her route*

**D.J.Joe** I thought you were on guard?

**Nesta** But you're here.

**D.J.Joe** Oh, yes. Alright.

*Marjory returns with her list and a box, finds D.J.Joe still
working, but thinking hard on what Nesta has said*

**D.J.Joe**  That old bird there is offering me money.
**Marjory**  Oh, yes?! You had better watch  yourself! I'll tell Mandy.
**D.J.Joe**  Don't be daft! For the business.
**Marjory**  For 'Nifty Shirts'?
**D.J.Joe**  Wants to invest seventy thousand.
**Marjory**  What!?
**D.J.Joe**  That's what she said.
**Marjory**  Never.
**D.J.Joe**  Honest.
**Marjory**  She's off her head.
**D.J.Joe**  'Nifty Shirts' is going places.
**Marjory**  Doesn't know what she's talking about.
**D.J.Joe**  Wants an income, she said.
**Marjory**  Well, there's better ways of getting an income than investing in your
    shop. You can't let her do it.
**D.J.Joe**  Why not?
**Marjory**  She might loose all her money. ... I don't  know though ... perhaps
    that's what she  deserves. Did you hear her going on about that poor Aunt
    of hers. All she's interested in was the poor old girl's money. It might serve
    her right if she lost it all with you.
**D.J.Joe**  What!
**Marjory**  I don't mean you'd misuse it, but she might find it tied up for a long
    time before she saw any return.
**D.J.Joe**  How would you know?
**Marjory**  Sorry, D.J., but I think you should steer clear. She'd be on your back
    the whole time.
**D.J.Joe**  Suppose so. Bad deal all round then?
**Marjory**  Just guessing. I'll have a word if you like, check it out.
**D.J.Joe**  Thanks. Oh shit! Think I'll put on  my  black  tie again.
**Marjory**  It's not that bad! And who cares about ties now. By the way I found this
    lot. *(hands him a box of black ties)*
**D.J.Joe**  Huh! Well... got excited for nothing...

*Sidney and Valerie return and dump stuff on the table once they
have thrown down some of the account books. D.J.Joe looks in
the boxes*

**D.J.Joe**  Is this all you could find? Bread and marmalade.
**Sidney**  Jim Taylor would have been pleased. Feast for him, bread and

marmalade.
**Valerie** I'll make sandwiches. Another drink anyone? *(she helps herself)*

*Nesta returns*

**Nesta** They are still there
**Valerie** Who?
**Nesta** The Police. I looked out of the Ladies window
**Sidney** Clever lady.
**Nesta** Thank you.

*They eat the sandwiches, all except Nesta who takes one look inside and puts it down*

**Marjory** Well. I've made my list. There's not a lot left. The coffee percolator's still there, so is the television...
**Sidney** Right, that will do for a start. Come on.

*Marjory ,Sidney and D.J.Joe leave*

**Valerie** You're quiet.
**Nesta** The funeral.
**Valerie** Made you think?
**Nesta** Yes.
**Valerie** Problems?
**Nesta** Perhaps.
**Valerie** Money?
**Nesta** What makes you think that?
**Valerie** People always think of money at funerals. They may be don't talk about it, but they all think about it. There's always money, or if there's no money there are 'things'. So everyone wonders who's getting it, how much, if those people need it and how they could use it better.
**Nesta** *(nervous smile)* Yes, I suppose you are right. I'd not thought of it myself.
**Valerie** No?
**Nesta** No.
**Valerie** Oh, well. ... I have to think about it. Since the divorce you see. now he's married again it might get difficult. He might not have the money to pay.
**Nesta** You could probably get a court order or something.
**Valerie** Not much use if he doesn't have the money.
**Nesta** You make sure you get it if you are entitled to it.
**Valerie** But I don't really need it now.
**Nesta** Everyone needs money.

**Valerie**  I've enough, I think. I work.
**Nesta**  Oh, I see. So do I of course.
**Valerie**  What do you do?
**Nesta**  Head of filing at Benson's.

*Marjory returns and works away in the background, overhears)*

**Valerie**  Benson's, I've heard of them. In fact, yes, we at Robertson and
       Robertson handled the sale of that big block of theirs on Dale Street.
**Nesta**  Oh? ... You're an estate agent?
**Valerie**  Assistant, just an assistant, but I love it.
**Nesta**  I might have a house to sell.
**Valerie**  Really ?
**Nesta**  My Aunt's.
**Valerie**  I see.
**Nesta**  Good area. Chatsworth Road.
**Valerie**  Big houses up there. Worth quite a bit.
**Nesta**  I thought so. About how much do you think?
**Valerie**  One forty, one fifty if you are lucky.
**Nesta**  As much as that.
**Valerie**  Oh yes.
**Nesta**  Thank you. Thank you very much.
**Valerie**  And remember Robertson and Robertson if you do decide to sell.
**Nesta**  I will. But this being shut in here is very annoying. I've so much to
       do. I think I'll go to the Ladies  and look.

       *Nesta has to squeeze past Marjory and Sidney carrying the
       coffee percolator and television*

**Sidney**  I'll plug it in over here I think.
**Marjory**  You'll be lucky.

       *Sidney grapples with the wiring system*

       Thank God she's gone.
**Valerie**  Not for long. She's spying on the Police.
**Marjory**  That woman! What a miserable person! I'm sorry I shouldn't speak like
       that about other guests. Money mad that one.

       *Sidney keeps trying with the wiring*

**Valerie**  She's a big house to sell on Chatsworth Road.
**Marjory**  Has she now?

**Sidney** Who's got a house on Chatsworth?
**Valerie** That woman, the one who was sitting here.
**Sidney** George's niece? His sisters house? No use. Poor woman.
**Marjory** What do you mean?
**Sidney** No use, have to be pulled down. Neglected over the years George says. That niece of his was banking on it apparently. Quite pushed. Made redundant from Benson's when the computers went in. Doesn't like anyone to know.
**Marjory** Oh, no. Poor woman. Redundant. I didn't know.
**Sidney** The land is worth something I suppose.
**Valerie** Not as much as the house in good condition. Anyway, leasehold. What a shame. I hate to see the old places come down. They'll build flats or a hotel or something. Big piece of land.
**Marjory** Where is it exactly?
**Sidney** Now Marjory! In your present state you can't go thinking of new sites.
**Marjory** I suppose not. ... It's D.J. I feel sorry for and he doesn't even know it!

*D.J.Joe returns and over hears*

**D.J.Joe** Why be sorry for me. I've got all my gear, quite safe.
**Marjory** Before this lot hit we were going to do up this place.
**D.J.Joe** So...
**Marjory** Thought of putting in some shop units.
**D.J.Joe** Yes...
**Marjory** Offering one to you for 'Nifty Shirts'.
**D.J.Joe** Whow!
**Marjory** But... *(sighs)* Sorry D.J. Shouldn't have mentioned it.
**D.J.Joe** Well... I'll just have to go in with the old woman then. Take on the shop next door. Put down some new carpet...

*Valerie has been quietly drinking and eating sandwiches. The mention of carpets attracts her*

**Valerie** I saw some nice carpet in a shop, now where was it...?
**Marjory** *(mock annoyed)* If you mention another item of furnishing, I'll...
**Valerie** You wouldn't hit me would you...?
**Marjory** No, no, I'm sorry.
**Valerie** Good. John only got away with it because...
**Marjory** You love the rotten bugger.
**Valerie** Yes...*(near to tears again)*
**Marjory** Oh, I'm sorry. Oh, God, I'm sorry.
**Valerie** That's alright. Marmalade sandwich anybody?

**Marjory** Well, I've done it all now. Made a guest cry. I've been most terribly
rude to that poor old woman.

*Nesta returns and overhears*

**Nesta** I am far from being a poor old woman. I paid you didn't I?
**Marjory** *(deep sigh)* Yes, yes, you paid me....

*Everyone is now listening to Marjory*

I think I've completely lost my touch. I'm never rude to a guest, I always keep
calm, I'm known for it, aren't I Sid? ... It's gone, gone completely. ... If I
have to be polite to another bloody idiot ... I'll burst.
**Sidney** It's O.K. Marj.
**Marjory** Oh Sid. Just look at those two. I was so rude!
**Sidney** They did push you a bit.
**Marjory** But it's my job to be polite! *(to the silent embarrassed company)* I am
very sorry. Sorry.

*Silence*

**Valerie** Marmalade sandwich anyone? Only watch the carpet, it's her
daughters you see.
**Nesta** No! And you're drunk!
**Valerie** But at least I'm not...
**Nesta** Not what?
**Marjory** Shut up!
**Valerie** Curtains are nice. Lovely pattern.

> *There is a knock at the door. complete silent attention. Sidney*
> *signals D.J.Joe to open it. The Man is standing outside*

**D.J.Joe** It's him!

*The Man steps into the room*

**The Man** I'd like to speak to Mrs Bainbridge, Mrs Marjory Bainbridge of the
Palace Hotel.
**Valerie** Oh! Halo!
**Marjory** *(standing up slowly)* I am Mrs Bainbridge.
**D.J.Joe** As if he didn't know.
**The Man** I have here a message from...
**Sidney** Get on with it man!

**Nesta**  Can we go now?
**Valerie**  The Anchor!
**The Man**  ... the court.
**Marjory**  Oh, no! They are under arrest!
**The Man**  Mr and Miss Bainbridge.
**D.J.Joe**  Yes?
**The Man**  Your husband and daughter, I believe?
**Marjory**  Oh, come on!
**The Man**  Have been released and are on there way here.
**Marjory**  Yes!!
**The Man**  As a consequence the goods are to be returned. On behalf of the
        Court and myself I would like to apologies for any inconvenience we may
        have, perhaps, caused.
**Marjory**  Thank you.
**The Man**  If you'll excuse me. I have to go and unload the lorry.
**Valerie**  I'll help.
**The Man**  That will be quite unnecessary Madame.
**Valerie**  *(trailing after him)* It's those chairs from the lounge - Smith and
        Plumpsteads.
**The Man**  So I believe Madame.
**Valerie**  Perhaps when you've finished you'd like to accompany me to the
        Anchor?
**The Man**  After we've done the Axminster perhaps...

> *They leave in an ecstasy of furniture talk. Nesta looks at her
> watch and begins the climb over the boxes*

**Nesta**  Four o'clock. Still time to get to the solicitors. If you'll excuse me.
**Marjory**  Of course Madame. Let me help you.

> *Nesta rejects the offer*

**Sidney**  Poor sod.
**D.J.Joe**  Now I can get my van. Will Angela and the rest get their jobs back?
**Marjory**  Of course, but it might take an hour or two!
**D.J.Joe**  Normal disco Saturday?
**Marjory**  Yes.
**D.J.Joe**  Shop unit??
**Marjory**  We'll see!
**D.J.Joe**  I'll get the van.

> *Marjory and Sidney are left in the chaos*

**Marjory** Oh Sid! Fancy your job in the bar back?
**Sidney** No, thank you! I can't wait to get back to the funeral. Then it's back to
the bank corner tomorrow.

*They have a hug and look at the chaos*

**Marjory** Oh Sid! And I promised I'd cope! ...Wait!

*Writes note*

**Sidney** What are you doing?
**Marjory** A note - to Bill and Rosemary.
**Sidney** But you'll see them...*(reads note)*
**Marjory** We need to celebrate
**Sidney** Meet me at the Anchor. Jim Taylor's funeral?
**Marjory** Yes! Come on!

*Black out*

# Technical, Set and Properties

**Sound**   Music to set the scene and get the action going, beginning of Act One
Music in Act one for the setting up of tables
Repeat of setting up music for end of Act One
Interval end. Music for start of Act Two
Music for end of Act Two.

**Lighting** Central area for both acts
Definite lighting for Funeral and Wedding areas, Act One
Reception in Act One and entrance for Act Two

**Act One** – The reception lounge of the hotel

Entrances to    Reception desk
Toilet
Funeral Reception
Kitchen
Bar
Wedding Reception

On stage        Small table with flowers, newspapers
Two chairs either side of the table
One upright chair opposite
Wedding and funeral areas with clothes and flowers

Props off       Trays of sandwiches, cutlery, napkins
Trays of drinks in paper cups
Flowers in funeral and wedding areas
Paper and pen
Huge pack of toilet roles
Shoe box of cruets
Note board, paper, pen

**Act Two** – Small office in another part of the hotel

Entrance to the rest of the hotel

On stage        Desk with office papers, dairies, hotel records
An ornament on the desk, box below
Chair for the desk
Electric fire and lead

Props off       Bread and marmalade, knife
Electrical wires and speakers
Boxes, all shapes and sizes
Bottles of drink
Box of ties
Flowers

# Other publications soon to follow from Green Light

All plays are new writing rehearsed and honed by actors before successful performances to appreciative audiences.

## Murder Mystery

Budd's Burning Question                    3M. 3F
    Building Development in a beautiful valley opens old family conflicts.


Mayhem at the Magpie                    3M. 3F
    Celebrity chef makes Christmas television programme


## Environmental Plays for Children and Family Audiences.

Phyllis,  the Frog and the Flea                    2M. 3F
    Our frog's pond is threatened by the building of a new road.


The Friends of Matty's Oak                    3M. 3F
    Matty's Oak wakes every 50 years when it faces a new man made danger